Little Bible Story Books

Baby

paternoster publishing

HUNT& THORPE

This is Mary.

This is Joseph.

This is the angel Gabriel.

God sent him to Mary.

Gabriel said Mary would soon have a baby, God's Son.

Then Gabriel went to Joseph.

He told Joseph to name the
baby, Jesus.

They went on a long journey
to Bethlehem.

There was no room for them
in the inn.

Jesus was born that night in
a stable.

Mary wrapped him up and laid
him in a manger.

In the hills there were
shepherds with their sheep.

Suddenly angels appeared.
The shepherds were frightened.

One angel said, "Don't be afraid.

We have good news. The Lord
Jesus has been born."

The shepherds went to look
for Jesus.

They found him in the stable
with the animals.

They praised God for the
wonderful things they had seen.

Far away in the East, a star appeared.

Some wise men saw it and
followed it to Bethlehem.

They brought precious gifts
and gave them to Jesus.

They were very happy to have found him.

You can read about the birth of Jesus in Matthew 1:18-2:23, and Luke 1:5-2:20.

First published by **Hunt & Thorpe** in the United Kingdom, 1990
ISBN 1-85608-040-4

The CIP catalogue record for this book is available from the British Library.

Hunt & Thorpe is a name used under licence by Paternoster Publishing, P.O. Box 300, Kingstown Broadway, Carlisle CA3 0QS

Manufactured in Singapore.

Reprinted 1997